Stars to Color

A Coloring Book for Adults & Children

By J.A. Ardis

For my mother.

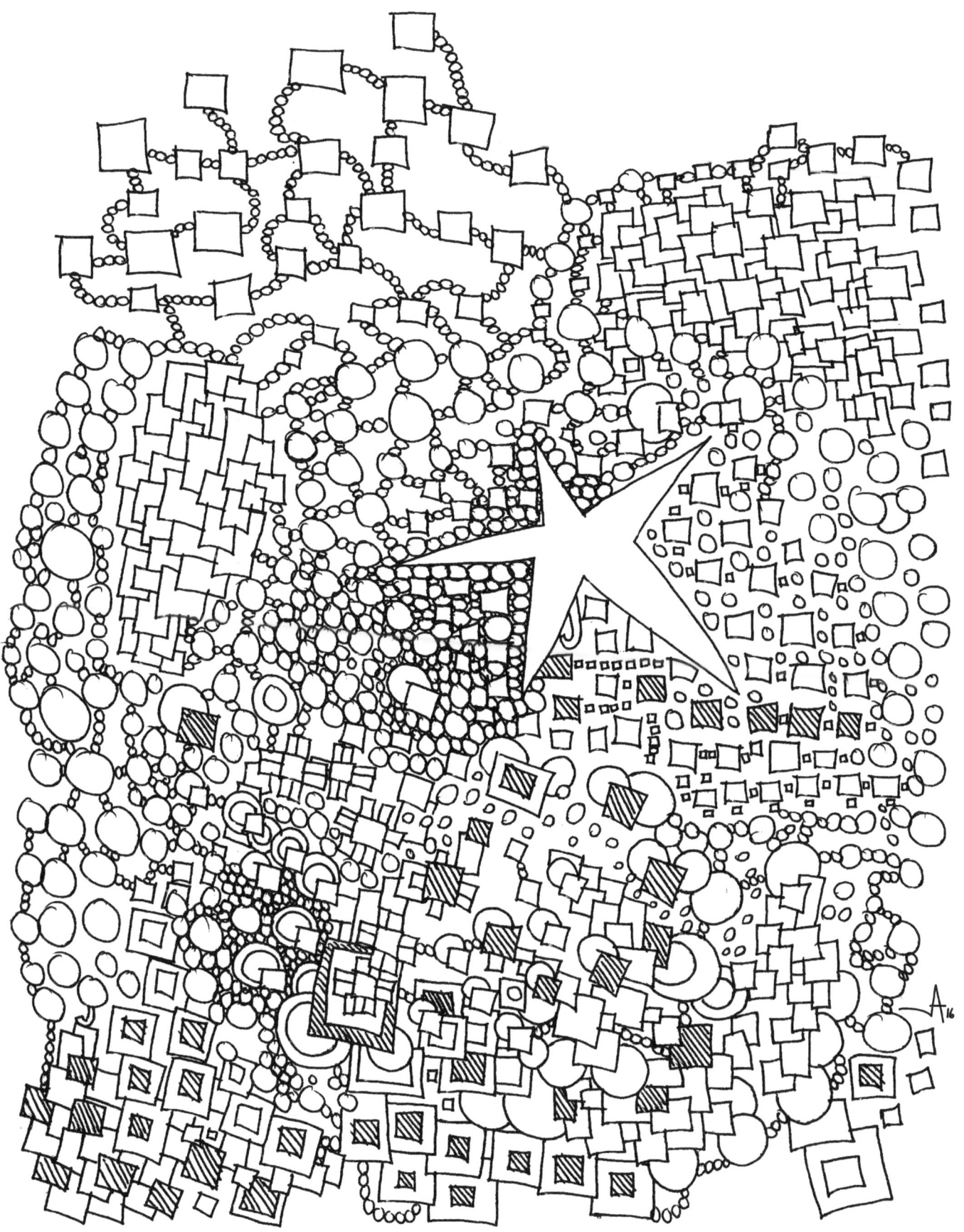

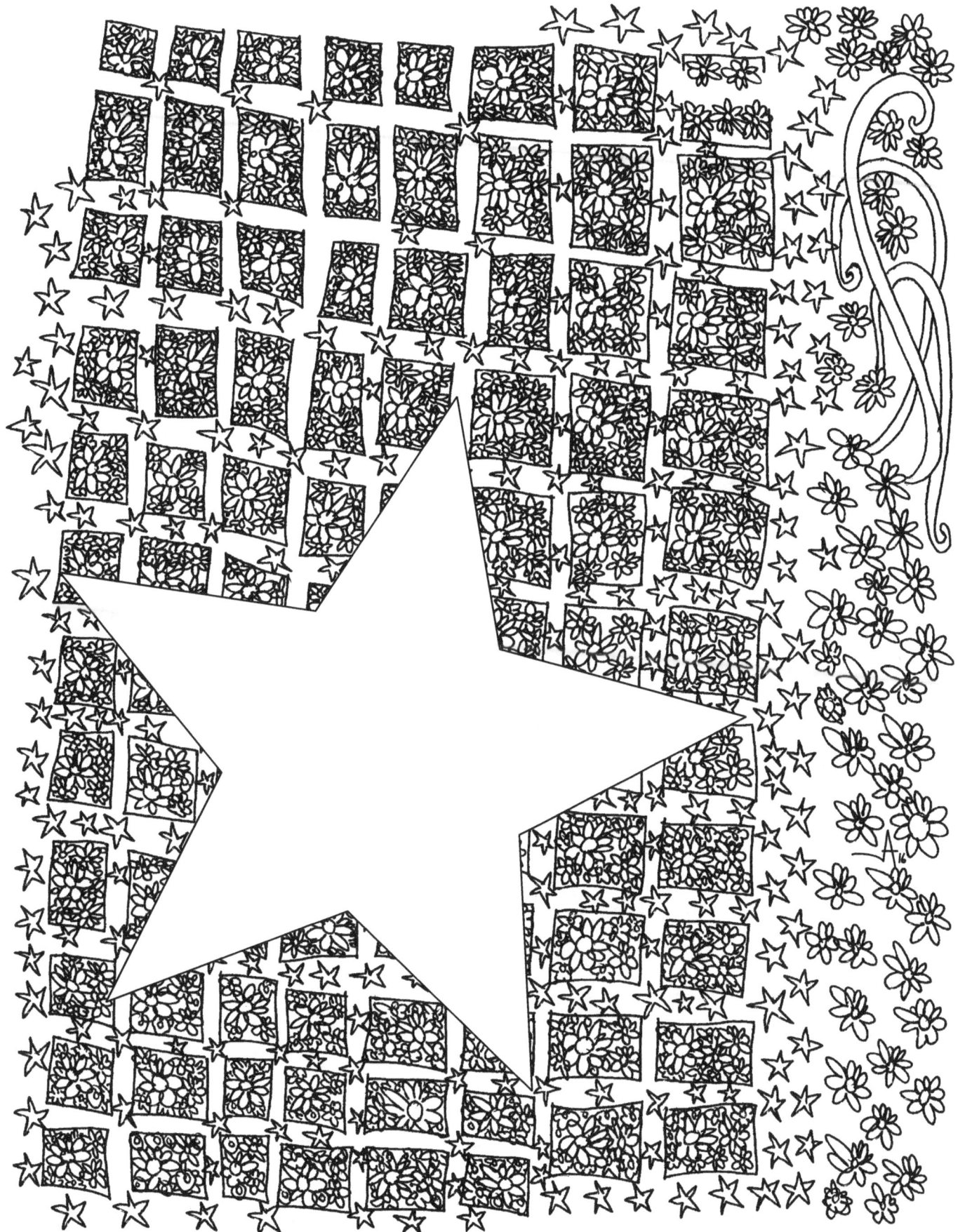

www.ingramcontent.com/pod-product-compliance
Lightning Source LLC
Chambersburg PA
CBHW080628190526
45169CB00009B/3321